A MIND NOT LOST
BOOK 2

Verona J. Knight

authorHOUSE®

AuthorHouse™ LLC
1663 Liberty Drive
Bloomington, IN 47403
www.authorhouse.com
Phone: 1-800-839-8640

Published by AuthorHouse 11/06/2013

ISBN: 978-1-4918-2938-7 (sc)
ISBN: 978-1-4918-2937-0 (e)

Library of Congress Control Number: 2013919422

A MIND NOT LOST Book 2
Book of Poetry
Words for the Mind

Verona J. Knight

CONTENTS

THE VAULT

(JUST THOUGHTS)—Foot Prints of my Mind

Dedicated to Love:

Found
Lost
Regained

DEAR HEAVEN

Dear Heaven . . . My mom has left and is now on her way
Please make her comfortable . . . Since she's there to stay
Let her meet up with her friends . . . that are already there
After her family finds her . . . they might not want to share

She has had a rough time in the past few years here
Now she's in your care . . . and had nothing before to compare
She always had your love . . . but . . . now she'll see your face
And that first feeling of touch . . . she will finally embrace

Hold her tight and help her with her steps
As she's a baby to heaven . . . and Father . . . You know best
And...until that day when I see your face also
I know she will learn as well . . . how to help me grow

I had cried for her journey when she first fell asleep
As she took a piece of my heart . . . but . . . it's hers to keep
And now as we've laid her down for her rest
Again I say Father . . . Only you know best.

Signed another of your daughters

INTRO

There are times when we have too much to say but without a voice. We cannot find the words to explain our thoughts. The voice to express what we feel is not there.

After years of enjoying life, thinking everything will be the same day after day, things changed. The happy days of watching my mom teaching her kids survival skills through her everyday life, gone. The days of my happy marriage pulled away by ill-willed hands and my days of good health moving to 'not so good'. Later finding out that my mind had a few volts missing from my memory charger. Things had changed.

I kept hearing stories of things that happened in my past, things I was a part of but didn't feel a part of. The special memories that should be a part of me, but wasn't. The important thing was that I wouldn't realised they were missing until brought to my attention in conversations. At first, if asked, I would say I don't remember but after a while I think I wasn't believed. After, I started pretending that I remembered but not contributing to that part of the conversation. I do remember more than I forgot but forgot some special parts; family events, friends gathering and vacation events.

Life changed. Illness took control of me and my marriage. After all of that, my memory couldn't remind me, I was scared. Then I started writing, for two reasons. The first because of personal relationship reasons and the other so I can go back and read my memories if anything happened. Now sometimes I read my writings and think how smart I sound and smile. I really enjoy reading my memory now.

AUTHOR'S NOTES

A MIND NOT LOST—Book of Poetry—Book 2 of 3 (Book 1 already on sale)

Book Two presents a collection of more than 100 pages of poems and thoughts that helped kept me strong and maybe can do the same for you; as others said helped them through. It's my thoughts on paper where I can re-read, to keep boosting my good thoughts and remind me of my strength on a daily basis. My thoughts of the day are included as they are ones that came to mind while observing and thinking about different situations and experiences in life; they have helped me through some turmoil in my live. These thoughts also remind me daily of the strength of my faith, the balance required to soothe each other's mind in a relationship, and of my sexuality.

Ease the Mind

GIFT OF WRITING

There are times in our lives
when we want to live free
**

But expressing our wants
is not as easy as it should be

***

Putting our thoughts on paper
makes us be what we want to be
**

We can rewrite . . . and rewrite
until we see whom we want to see

*****

A beautiful mind
going . . . to different places
**

Mingling with different people
hearts . . . and races

***

To sculpture a world . . . in one's own imagination
**

Be whomever . . . doing whatever
without . . . ramification

*****

That world where fantasy can be so real
And that reality is all you want to feel

***

If there are no easy way
to express your heart
**

Speak to your paper
and . . . it will give you a start

*****

When troubles of your heart . . . or mind
feels unwanted
*

The gift of writing
should never be taken . . . for granted.

CHILD BIRTH

I look at my baby today
And would not have believed
*

That one who inflicted such pain
Would've given me any relief

*****

To experience the twisting . . . screaming
And what feels . . . like the agony of defeat
*

The cussing . . . the blaming
Then the head . . . shoulders . . . and those little feet

*****

My heart now fills with joy
And all swearing have subside
*

For many years have passed
And good memories are left inside

*****

To see my baby walk away
Not knowing what to expect
*

To do some swearing of her own
I know for me it'll strengthen her respect.

KARMA

He's been mine for a good while now
*

Joy filled my heart . . . but reality takes a bow
**

My mind was worried . . . but
thinking good thoughts
*

'Cause we looked so happy
but I might be losing his heart

*****

As she walks close to stand by his side
*

His gaze that swallows her . . . couldn't hide

Standing . . . pretending to be a stranger
*

Thinking her charade . . . causes . . . no danger
**

Reality screams out that 'something isn't right!'
*

We stood . . . his essence beams . . . delightfully bright

****

Her heart enjoying pleasures . . . at my cost
*

Me . . . standing . . . with such great feelings of loss
**

His hand she passed and touched . . . lightly
*

His body reacts . . . even though . . . just slightly

*****

I'm troubled but mostly hates the fact
*

She touched then went . . .
Thinking it was behind my back
**

I struggle whether to confront
since I'm bent
*

But reality holds my mouth
Saying . . . karma must vent

KARMA. You're really such a BITCH . . .
*

But was I really once that witch?

****

What we send out in life is what we invite to ours. What goes around comes around.

LIFE

Every day we awake
to the greatest present anyone can get
*

Many take it for granted
not knowing the appreciation of it yet

***

We'll all travel different paths
but with the same accessories
*

The ability to use our mind and soul
to say/do what is necessary

***

So make life's comfortable abilities
be a precious gift
*

And enjoy life and appreciate
the presence of our gift

***

Don't waste your time consumed
with another person's life
*

Don't criticise others
showing you think yours not a special life

***

If you want to talk
do something worth talking about
*

Don't watch others be
what you want to . . . without any doubt

***

It's said . . . someone not willing to learn . . .
is worse than those . . .
*

Without the ability to learn . . .
if they're not able to let knowledge impose

****

Learn from them and move forward. If you're happy with your life you
won't have time to spend watching another live theirs so to criticise.

LOVE YOU

I miss you baby now
I missed having you baby, back then
*

I'll miss you baby if you're not mine
I might miss you 'till forever . . . I just can't tell me when

***

BUT
That IN-LOVE has left and gone
*

So now is when . . . I must move on
***

Love doesn't plant its seeds
Then stay for every season
*

So see me and know . . . that
everything happens for a reason

*****

*****

Because you broke my heart
*

That's not any reason to fall apart
***

Moping and losing my identity

*

Isn't where to start finding stability
***

I love you baby now
I loved you baby . . . back then
*

I will love you baby after this
I'll love you . . . just don't know . . . 'till when

****

*****

Often our love for someone prevents us from moving on when it's over. But we must love ourselves enough to know how to move away towards better.

MY PAIN I CLAIM

The harshness of your mind
comes easily from your mouth
*

The ignorance of my mind
recognises not . . . what it's all about

**

The memories of my nightly aches for you
are now in remission
*

Knowing those nights my love was given
to another without my permission

**

Daily . . . you package my love then taking it to your date
*

My dedication to you . . . now bows
my package filled with hate

**

Your breath
sprays my face with vicious words of distaste
*

And my body . . . you paint with words of blame
with such haste

**

My blame I do accept for my part in your pain
*

Your part you now see
Will . . . jeopardise your life's gain

**

With the malicious words from your lips
so coldly peeling
*

Take all your faults . . . unclaimed
to help me with my healing

**

You made your decision
to
make love to another
*

Taking my rights
by not using precaution
with your other

**

With all that said I now roll up my sleeve
*

To fight . . . for my future . . . right after you leave

**

Don't sigh . . . 'cause I won't cry

*

Just take a step back . . . as I say . . .
'GoodBye'

****

When the love we think of as ours is given to another the trust is taken away with the action. When you find out then the blame comes on you why it happened and with what they get they also carries back to you without your say.

MY TREASURE CHEST

HOPE...
for the bright future yet to come

**

STRENGTH...
for enduring anything and then some

**

DETERMINATION...
to fight to accomplish

**

LIFE'S LESSON...
from the heartache and whatever was dished

**

SURVIVAL...
from the pain I now can shield

**

HEARTACHE...
to which I survived and didn't yield

**

SURVIVING LOSS...
of some dear to me

**

FRIENDSHIP . . .
in many I didn't know but now see

**

SUPPORT . . .
to those who shares my journey

**

EXPERIENCE . . .
to guide others on their journey

*

ADVICE . . .
I can tell of where I've been

**

HELP . . .
to help guide those heading into the unseen.

**

Please feel free to help yourself . . .
I learned the hard way myself . . .
**
Blessings

******

Our blessings are there even when we don't remember them.

WASTED TIME

All we need is to find our inner strength
*

To know in life when to . . . and when not to vent

*****

Our Creator
does not play favourites with any of us
*

By making some special
while to others . . . not so generous

*****

Think about life and how many times we've felt pain
*

Falling on our face . . . heartache
and even . . . driving our self insane

*****

Now think about the fear that accompanied each situation
*

Think about the memories
and how they now need no attention

*****

There are things in life we will be afraid to do

*

*But must ask the Creator to help
and walk us through*

*****

*Look back over them years
and you will see what had been*

*

*You'll see your time wasted on
what wasn't as bad as it was seen*

****

What seems bad today might not look so bad tomorrow.

HIT AND MISS

Intelligence said
I know what to do . . . 'cause . . . I can read the signs
***

Smarts said
I know how to do . . . you just stay behind
***

The heart said
You both think you do . . . but I won't let you through
***

If I leave it up to you
I'll feel nothing but blue

*****

The soul need to speak
So it sends messages to the mind
***

The mind tries to come up with a way
To say 'be kind'
***

With the right words saying to speak from the heart
***

The heart changes then do the wrong
After . . . needs another start

*****

Back to the drawing board we go . . .
Now with some anger
***

The mind and the soul can't take this any longer
***

With all the talk and decisions made before
***

The heart keeps going its own way
Getting beat . . . then sore

*****

How much longer can we do this?
Now even the heart is getting piss
***

I'm tired of doing this
Always a hit . . . and miss
***

The more I feel hurt
The more I still can't resist

*****

The heart wants what the heart wants
***

It doesn't want to hear anything
That sounds like can't
***

It cares nothing about intelligence or being smart
***

It can't get beyond itself
Not even if . . . it means a re-start

*****

It thinks it knows best
But nothing is further from the truth
***

So it hurts and hurts
Leaving intelligence and smart to help re-boot
***

The heart . . . always making a mess
***

Leaving a heavy struggle for the rest
***

Over . . . and over . . . giving the test
***

But . . . one day it will realize
That it doesn't know best

****

When we follow the heart into trouble, we make excuses why not to follow good sense.

O HE/SHE CHEATS

There are times in most of our lives
*

Whether a mother . . . father . . . husband or wife
*

When we need . . . to take a safe step back
*

So not to trip over anyone's . . . made-up fact
*

The painful branding . . . from your guilt
and wilful attempts
*

You think will leave me hurting
Stopping my accusations . . . in all events

***

I . . . like you . . . have had my eyes on someone too
*

But I didn't want to go forward just to . . . cheat on you
*

Though some will have people
coming in and out of their life
*

I keep my distance
Leaving me thinking . . . about my will to strive
*

Knowing what will cause one's body
and good sense
to be confused
*

Your thoughts
should have seen the value placed
on what you can lose

***

But . . . I'm glad you went ahead
taking the first step
digging your hole so deep
*

Now I'll have no guilt
of whom I haven't yet slept
or will someday sleep

****

Because your partner haven't cheated doesn't mean they haven't thought about it. Some are smarter than others and not take a chance of losing what they have while others are weak and only think about it all after the act.

Awaken your Sensuality

A REAL MAN

We sometimes go through our day
Just wanting to see the end
***

Not seeing beyond today
And with our spirits bend

*****

While in heightened passion
loving comes prematurely
And makes us lie
***

Having me pretending it was good
But inside . . . we just need to cry

*****

The fake love we sometimes feel
Is somehow seen as real
***

But the heart that should comfort
Has almost lost its appeal

*****

Since laying wide opened welcoming
Your voice says something nice
***

When really it's broken by confused love
That somehow is lacking enough spice

*****

Then . . . a real man comes along . . . with
Orgasmic forces . . . thinking 'damn . . . he's good'
***

And you finally know how it feels
To have a blanket of getting it real good

*****

Just like mice . . . feeling . . . enjoying the nibbles
***

Breast swelling . . . wet peeping . . . O . . . them nipples

*****

Feeling them fingers
Playing tic-tac-toe with them parts
***

Goodness . . . Gracious
Your whole world is hugging his heart

*****

Riding the axles of them hips
Searching and finding the love seek
***

Climbing the mounts of ecstasy
Thrusting and keeping . . . at the peek

*****

Balancing the zone of painful . . . and pleasure
Creeping . . . inside . . . looking to unload
***

Into that secret place of yours
He crawls . . . and . . . meet . . . to explode
Pleasurably . . . accompanying . . . each other . . . unload

****

Some fake it to avoid hurting feelings then go elsewhere to find what they seek for healing

BENEATH

This love from you got me going
*

This body of mine is hungry
Almost flowing
***

***

The memories of your touch
engulfing my mind
*

Kisses slivers down my body
touching all it find
****

****

Ooo . . . you're . . . touching me
down there
*

My senses are confused
Mmm . . . pulling . . . my hair
***

***

My juices are flowing
in search of places to go
*

Fingers feeling. Going where?
I'm too confused to know

****

Oh how my body shivers
Mmmn . . . my breast . . . your lips
*

Forsaking any reservation
taking your body in . . . my hips
***

***

Haven knows
I care not for anything else about now
*

My body twisting
Feeling you deep inside me . . . wow

*****

Holy shit! You hit it!
O gosh! That spot!
*

Just keep giving it
Everything you got
***

***

O goodness
how your body taste like wine
*

My inside tasting juices
Painting and splashing my loin

****

Our bodies relaxes . . . after stiffening
*

Mine says . . . 'thank you for

Everything . . . yours was giving'
***

***

Easing my way
Crawling . . . slowly from beneath
*

I breathe relief
for having something so sweet

****

Your work reminding me
this pleasure need not end
*

Between my legs saying
Please make him my best friend
***

While my mind says . . . 'we sure must do this again'
***

How divine.
Them signs.

I SEE HIM

I see my future
Looking . . . fine enough to consume
**

Plans changing
as he was sent for me . . . I presume

****

To touch him . . . caress him
taste him . . . like testing wine
**

My body's reaction says
I'm sure he would feel divine

****

My legs . . . I must cross
when he comes closer
looking to pass
**

Then he squeezes by
giving me a glimpse
of some really fine ass

****

The pressure building excitement
Admiring . . . I see his chest

**

Matching the turmoil inside me
I feel lips sliding . . . VJJ . . . making a mess

****

Today emotions concurring . . . now years passed by
showing my work wasn't in vain
**
We now stand before God
saying the words again and again

****

To love and to honour
for better or for worse
**
Till death do us part
All . . . without any haste

****

The intensity of our love
spills daily from our hearts
**
To tell us that this love
will be . . .
'never torn apart'.

MEET DICK

Although attractive . . . not very wise
*

Put lots of work into
being thought of a prize
*

Even though bald . . . Dick is never shy
*

Sometime needs to compete
when should say bye
*

Always takes pride . . . in making friends fast
*

Mostly not wanting . . . those friendships to last

***

Dick enjoys travelling . . . finding new territories for admiring

***

Sometimes like travelling with others
*

And sometimes envy the travels of others
*

Dick's major fear is only the wife
*

Finding out about the secret life

*

Always taking pride
in standing manly strong
*

Not concerned about anything
Unexpectedly going wrong

*

One day . . . Dick notice something wasn't right
*

Dick needs a little help standing . . . didn't have the bite
*

Dick can't tell friends
about needing help with strength
*

Did finally get some help
But for how much time . . . no length

*

Dick's head now allows the lips to do everything
*

Then stop since the lips comforter wears his ring
*

Dick decides to spend more time with the wife
*

Using her help . . . figuring things out about his life
*

After a while Dick's need to travel taunts
*

While needing to do outside research haunts

*

Dick finds something that can help him go
extra
*

Dick enjoys travelling but now . . . can only travel
VIA-GRA.

***

Dick no longer travels with a limp
But needs his pills as his pimp

MY BODY—YOUR HEART

Kiss me . . . caress me . . . mmm . . .

your hands

rolling me . . . holding me . . . penetrating . . .

my body

hurting . . . aching . . . crying . . .

for you only

can ease my pain

*****

Protect me . . . explore me . . .

slowly

your entry . . . your touch . . . enjoy . . .

your tongue

tasting me . . . teasing me . . . gliding over . . .

my moist lips

trembling eagerly

*****

Invade me . . . break me . . . violate . . .

my womb

moving . . . painfully enjoying . . .

you

are infectious . . . your emotions . . . your love . . .

twisting my body

slowly . . . crawling . . . elevating . . .
to heaven . . .

YOUR FEEL

Your feel . . . .
O . . . how my body takes pleasure there
*

Your memory . . . .
Yes . . . it linger even when . . . you're not here
*

Your touch . . . .
I crave with every thought . . . and feel
*

Your love . . . .
I treasured . . . to come when I need to heal
*****

*****

My body . . . .
Hurt . . . with thoughts of you with . . . another
*

My mind . . . .
Confused the present and the past . . . never
*

My heart . . . .
Pressured . . . from the love I've lost
*

My thoughts . . . .
Pains my feelings . . . that was a cost
*****

*****

Your love . . . .
Given another's heart . . . warmth . . . safely
*

My love . . . .
Sits wondering . . . if to move on . . . or not . . . bravely
*

Your mistake . . . .
You see no faults but only caress blame
*

My mistake . . . .
Trusting what you told my heart . . .
Over and over again
*****

*****

Your actions . . . .
Speaks louder . . . than your words
*

Showing in your life
My lack of worth
*

Again . . . actions . . . .
Speaks louder . . . than your words
*

Your lengths to go to another
Tells me your thought of their worth

CARELESS HABITS

Who are you? And where did you come from?
*
Watching so intensely, looking like you want some
**
A stranger . . . but yet . . . you seem so familiar
*
A stranger who . . . could slowly . . . turn me into a liar.

***

You watching . . . I'm looking . . . so intensely
*
No words . . . eyes saying . . . 'craven you immensely'
**
Would I want to do something . . . knowingly wrong?
*
Just for the pleasures from . . . a one night stand

***

From deep inside . . . . corrupted . . . . that feeling
*
Help! My mind already knows . . . . the ending
**
Is it worth it? What? You know . . . cheating!
*
Bad sense says 'after once you won't be repeating'

****

Now, this quiet walk, to meet in the middle
*

Thinking this way, we'll both . . . . be chancing a little
**

Without a doubt my panty . . . is . . . tasting some sweat
*

Tease my senses! My legs give in . . . Mercy . . . I'm wet.
****

Mercy, mercy! Your touch . . . the needle I need to feel
**

You are the one with . . . my medicine . . . that is ideal.

****
****

Now with my memories looking back
once turned us into each other's habit
**

Knowing it all one day would come undone
Uncontrollably acting like stupid rabbits

***

Now feeling the daily pleasures coming
From conveniently having my man
**

Turning to the sexual frustration
Forcing my role . . . playing . . . with my hand
**

The misplaced trust now haunts my mind
Oh . . . my heart is broken

**

The heart that is mine . . . got careless
Now . . . got stolen

***

Without the calm
I've carelessly created the storm
**

Because I craved the other
my true love . . . is . . . now . . . gone

Soothes the Soul

ASK LIFE

If you want to know the meaning of life
The best way to know is . . . to ask life

*****

The answers might not see you through
But there'll be no answers . . . by asking you

*****

From the carefree years of youth
you couldn't wait to leave
To the teenage years of innocence
teaching what you couldn't believe

*****

The day your body changed over into
womanhood
And was also taken advantage of
by one's manhood

*****

The day your love . . . came to you wandering
And your inside changed . . . after you let him in

*****

When you gave your heart on that platter
He took yours . . . and . . . also went on to another

*****

The pain from child birth . . . moving on to rearing
Going to the loneliness of . . . single parenting

*****

The willingness to move on . . . to enjoy another
While burdened memories . . . handcuffs you to the other

*****

The overwhelming . . . awful . . . feelings of despair
When in the end . . . finding . . . there's nobody there

*****

I asked life 'Why me?
What did I ever do to you?'
It answered
'You were the strongest I had to turn to'

*****
*****

What else in life could I have been?
Away from all the things . . . I have seen

*****

***

A life with no hurdles . . . and troubles along the way
Ending up weak . . . and . . . with nothing to teach or say

Hard lessons . . . but I now know how to strive
I loved the answer received . . . when I Asked Life

DEAR FATHER

Dear Father, please take my hand
I ask that you hold me, when I stand
*

Every day, every hour
I need you to show me the light
*

When I go to sleep
I'll keep you with me through the night

****

I feel weak and pressured . . . can't hold on
Father please . . . help me . . . to carry on
*

My heart is but torn
O Father . . . my body is all so worn

****

****

I've tried to help myself through
But my efforts are no good without you
*

Help me Lord through this storm
Please Father . . . just keep me warm

****

I thought I over came on my own before
But now I know better, I can't do it anymore

*

I know now that You were always with me
For in my heart . . . You've been and will always be

****

****

Father again, I will never give up
Hold my hand and assist me to stand up

*

In my walk . . . I believe I won't be alone
I know You'll never leave me on my own

****

But Father, I still ask you again
Please, protect me . . . . Amen

IMPERFECTIONS

In your eyes . . . I may not look as sweet
You might even see my . . . crooked teeth
***

*

You might see my face as being too round
Promise . . . I still don't walk with a frown
***

*

My walk might not even be as stylish
But I walk with confidence . . . not anguish
***

*

You may even see my hand as too short
But it embraces my Father's love . . . in my heart
***

*

My body might not be well proportioned
But . . . that's not as important . . . to be mentioned
***

*

My body might not look as good as yours do
*

But I have no inferiority complex
standing beside you
***

*

The Father made us all in our own way

*

See . . . what works for you now
might stop working some day
***

*

I'm blessed with the ability
to see through to what's to come

*

But only . . . you concentrate on now
Thinking . . . the future won't come

MAMA

Mama . . . . where are you?
Mama . . . . what did I do?

***

Mama . . . . where did you go?
Mama . . . . I do miss you so

***

Mama . . . . I wish you could see
Mama . . . . I just can't let you be

***

Mama . . . . it's not fair to me
Mama . . . . don't let me be

***

Mama . . . . I can be selfish . . . as you know
Mama . . . . I just don't know how to let you go

***

Mama . . . . I can't stand this any longer
Mama . . . . I try not to give in, to this anger

***

Mama . . . . my heart is torn
Mama . . . . O . . . . my body is worn

***

Mama . . . . right now . . . . I'm very sad
Mama . . . . it's Ok . . . . go . . . . be with God

MY JUDGE

My judge and jury of this world
cannot sentence me to damnation
*

But be careful, criticism of others
might jeopardise their own salvation.
***

I've seen the hands of the devil
and all the pain it brought to me
*

So I appreciate the hands of my Father
and His plans He has for me.

*****

As a child my mom reminded me
'The Father giveth and He taketh away'
*

As an adult I know that, we, make the mess
and throw it all away.
***

***

The Father gives much and we abuse
causing the 'lost'
*

Sometimes without realizing the severity
and at what cost.

*****

Ask for forgiveness and move away
from that threatening situation
*

Not for forgiveness then carry on
and be threatened by a situation.
*

I'm working for my Father's favour
not that of any man's
*

I'm protected . . . highly favoured . . . and covered
by my Father's hands.

THE CALL

I asked the Father to protect me
from back biters . . .
I asked Him to help me be
a better fighter . . .
*

Any weapons that may be formed against me . . .
I asked for His help to let me see . . .
*

Then I tell my friends I don't need anyone . . .
That I don't need them to keep me strong . . .
*

But Father, only you know my thoughts . . .
So You allowed no human . . . to slay my heart . . .
*

Clarification is where my actions come in . . .
For every move I make . . . I ask You to come in . . .

***

The path of darkness
is where too many are heading . . .
You're keeping me safe
by allowing me to see the unseen . . .
*

I tell them You have always walked with me . . .
I tell them I do see things they cannot see . . .
*

I tell them I was prepared
for the path of righteousness . . .
I said they can also be
if
they haven't been yet . . . . . . yes.

THE ANSWER

The Father is my Shepard
so I've never walked alone
*

Even when I didn't know Him
He watched from His throne
*

For every time I called His name
even just as a gesture
*

He stood and covered me
and my loyalty He didn't measure
**

For everyone that call upon Him
shall get His attention
*

Not stopping to see if it was He
you meant to call on
*

We are simple beings
created for a mission
*

Special . . . can be highly favoured
loved with such passion

*****

Nothing on this earth is worth more
We entered in a way some might think poor

*

The richness of that first breath
is what we seek
*

To leave with the same love
is the richest peak
*

Now treasure that love like it's your gold
*

Make sure it last when you grow cold
***

For even as sinners we
call on His name
*

But ignore His call when
He does the same.
******

***

Many know the Father only when they need Him.

The Vault

between chapters from
"The Cheaters, The Wife, The Revenge"
By: Verona J. Knight

FORGIVENESS

Sorrow came to my door
And I told him to go away

*

Pity . . . accompanied him
I also asked him not to stay

*

Vengeance was there waiting
I also . . . suggested he leave

****

Strength . . . and endurance
Will be on which I will cleave

*

Forgiveness was watching
Waiting to see what I would say

*

I looked then asked . . . calmly
For him to . . . kindly bring me some relief

****** ******
******

Thinking before acting is the best way to make little mistakes.

BABY PLEASE

Baby please love me . . .
    If only just for being me

        I'm trying my best to be . . .
          The man you want me to be

**

        Take my love and please . . .
          Enjoy it with confidence

          All the trust and admiration . . .
            I do now give . . . as evidence

**

My love for you is strong . . .
    And I know to you . . . it does belong

        Since your love for me I thought was gone
          I do . . . now see . . . was still there all along

**

Always take pride
  In your strength that you possess

      You will always have my love . . .
      And I do promise you . . . no regress

                ****** ******

We shouldn't try to change someone into who we want them to be
after choosing them for what they are.

DECISIONS

I was pissed yesterday
As angry caressed me
*

I'm so lonely today
My body needs love

******

I'll be calm tomorrow
To welcome a new day
*

Emotional decisions
I cannot . . . take my way

******

I won't depend on angry
'Cause he . . . is just a bully
*

I won't depend on lonely
'Cause he . . . is only for himself

******

I will look to calm though
'Cause it is easy to see
*

That he . . . is the only one
Looking out . . . only for me

DON'T CRY

Never you cry
for a love that you have lost
*

Especially . . . if it was given
to another at . . . your cost

**

Never put someone's ego
up . . . high on the throne
*

While your self-esteem
was left in the gutter . . . to drown
*

The pain . . . the misery . . .
The emptiness you feel
*

The pity . . . and blame . . .
Wasn't a part of the deal

**

Their joy from your pain
watching you go insane
*

Is good for their ego
While . . . you have nothing to gain

*

Lift up your spirits and
sing a brand new hymn
*

And let it be known to all
that you didn't die for her/him

**

One day they will see
the price paid
for their pain
*

For letting you become
someone's
other than their gain

******

****

Lifting someone's ego should never be more
important than your self-esteem.

GOOD FRIENDS

We go through our struggles
Always fighting hard to stay strong

******

Hoping to come out stronger
Than even when we began

******

Having good friends beside us
To give us a helping hand

******

Will be the making difference
In how long . . . we will stay strong

******

Good friends are very dear
And very good friends . . . are very rear

******
****

Never take friends for granted.

HAPPINESS

He has shown me great happiness
*
Recently also given me . . . a taste of hell

**

I've also enjoyed my share of happiness
*
On my experiences . . . I decided not to dwell

****

Though I don't strive to be perfect
I do strive for perfection
*
Striving towards a better me
is my only intention

******

One day as I looked through my window
*
my heart felt so much joy to see

**

That all of my haunting bad feelings
*
Were ready to turn their backs on me

******

****

When we dwell on our hurt we have no time to dream happy.

I PLEDGE

I will pledge my love to you . . . now
I will pledge my love to you . . . forever

*****

I did not say it to you then
But . . . don't doubt my love again . . . never

****

My heart . . . yes . . . the feelings are all real
My emotions . . . no . . . sometime I couldn't deal

*****

I've had your love now
for a long time
*
No words were said
But . . . you've always had mine

****

My thoughts . . . engulfing my mind with you
My greatest wealth . . . knowing you think of me too

*****

I will guard your heart . . . from anyone's wrong
'Cause . . . Your love is all . . . that is keeping me strong

****

*****

Sometimes when we lose trust in someone, we can start over
and give another chance so not to say 'what if' later.

MISSING

He sees me like I'm not even there
**

I often wonder . . . if he remembers my name
**

I see him and wonder . . . if he himself is there
**

Since his face I can see is fading here

*****

He drives by her house . . . to make sure she's ok
**

Then comes home to me . . . and pretend he's ok
**

Curiosity insisted I ask . . . if she's prettier than me
**

He held me tight . . . and said . . . that could never be

*****

I look at him, thinking the future might be bright
**

For in my heart I still hope, he will see the light
**

I'll be here for a while, and I'll take comfort in

**

That in someone else's heart, my picture will be seen

******

****

Some people stay together, for the wrong reasons,
and pretend they're happy, for the wrong reasons
and ending up stifling each other's life.

NEW YEAR

Goodbye last year . . .
You were very mean to me
*

Hello present . . .
You are the best sight to see

***

Welcome New Year
You feel good . . . now . . . make love to me
*

Mmmm . . . Yes . . . Good
Now please stay with me

***

Good morning yesterday
How are you doing today?
*

I'm feeling hopeful
Even though it's only been a day

***

Please . . . just stay strong for me
You will . . . have a big role to play
*

Anyway . . . let's talk about it later
We'll just have to take it day . . . by . . . day

*****

*****

There's always a year when things didn't go as planned so
make plans again to make it right in the new year.

TIME

It is said that time
will change everything
*

But without personal changes
It will mean nothing

******

For time to make changes
We must work with it
*

So we'll recognize any difference
Even if it's just a bit

******

Make all your changes
With high expectations
*

Then watch and pray
As change comes along

******

For a brighter future
Dwelling will never help
*

Charge forward . . . and if needed
Ask for some help
******

****

We can't do the same things and expect different results.

I WILL ALWAYS

Always . . .
Thanking The CREATOR for my blessings

***

Always . . .
Thanking The CREATOR for my todays

***

Always . . .
Thanking The CREATOR for my dark yesterdays

***

Always . . .
Asking The CREATOR for my bright tomorrows

***
***

I Will
Always . . . acknowledge my blessings

***

I Will
Always . . . and forever cherish my todays

***

I Will

Always . . . learn from my dark yesterdays

***

I Will

Always . . . praise . . . my CREATOR . . . for all my tomorrows

GOOD DARKNESS

I sat watching him as my mind drifted away
*
His body was there . . . but my heart could not stay

****

I lay in his arms sometimes
but each night and day I pray
*
Then I picture him there
and those thoughts flood my way.

****

Too many . . . dark yesterdays . . . he has created for me
*
They're shaping all tomorrows . . . into better ones to be

****

Polish each today so to shine
like they never have before
*

Then pat yourself on the back
then rejoice again once more.

******

******

We should use our pain to fuel our drive to the future.
Learn from mistakes and turn them into lessons.

GOODBYE HEARTACHE
HELLO HEART

Goodbye to my heartache
And hello happy . . . my old friend
**

It is so nice for me to know
I have finally caught up with you again
******

For such a long time now
I have turned my back on you
*****

But I am relieved to know
That you did not do the same too

******

I ask that you stay close to me
So you will not be out of my view
*****

Because heartache is a drug
That will somehow overpower you

******

I will correct the intake of my mind
So everything I feel falls into place
**

For the results of our thoughts
Are from the good we do in case

******

****

After the break-up comes the self-pity mode. Then one day you realise you were happy before them and gain your strength again.

Just a Thought

Foot Prints of My Mind

JUST A THOUGHT
He Explained My Dream

***

One night I had a dream that I was driving on a deserted road
somewhere
I recognised the place but without warning, I was walking towards
a stream; waters unclear
*

I was now with my husband both walking with a tour guide
'Nowhere to cross.' By looking at the water it was too deep from
that side
*

The guide threw a few coins into the water; reasons I didn't know
While we watched, he told us to wait; the water will stop its flow
*

Telling us the spot where it's the best to cross, will get clear
A little while after we moved closer but, still with some fear
*

Finally it cleared in one spot, ten feet wide and became shallow
But close to the other side had a crater looking deep; like it's able to
swallow

*

At first I was scared . . . But for me that's not weird
But the guide showed me how to cross and how to leap
Things like that I can only do in my sleep
*

He said to keep my feet crawling on the bottom
Why he trusted me to do it, I couldn't fathom
*

Said when I get to the crater, just use the force of my legs and leap
But I didn't know I was asleep, and with my fear, I couldn't leap
But, I did it as my husband watched . . . waiting for his turn
My fear intensified . . . I landed as my feet felt burn

*

I awoke with my heart racing . . . . Still my fears were chasing
*

As everyone who knows me, know I don't like height
That's when I called to God to awake me . . . from such fright
*

I entered in my journal before I went back to sleep
Even though scary . . . my memory . . . I wanted to keep
*

Next morning, thinking about my dream . . . my mind still tangled
in a knot
Without talking to anyone I felt/believe the tour guide . . . my
angle I got
*

The voice in my head explaining 'don't make decisions with a
cloudy mind'
Stand firm on the ground, see clearly before I leap seeking to find
That way I can survive the craters before me I can see
I just thank my FATHER for sending his guide to message me

*

With all that in mind, I must confess
My mind really was fearful . . . to take its rest
But with this thought . . . fear won't visit me anymore
I've never had an experience like this, never before
*

Even in my sleep I'm protected.
I had to share.

94

The Perfect Being

***

We sometimes forget what we want in a mate
Then with each little problem we only find things to hate
*

Look for our perception of what we think we should want
Then look at him/her thinking you can change them . . . but can't
*

Instead of first seeing that the person is not gonna be right for you
Expecting to make happy in your relationship that you alone might not do
*

But keep looking for that person you want and don't play blind
Don't stop at what you think you can create, from what you find

*****

To all those looking for the perfect man/woman . . . he/she doesn't exist
Know that trouble is a normal part of life . . . no matter what you can't resist
*

Avoid disappoints by not expecting more than they have to give
Expecting more doesn't mean they have the ability to find more to give
*

From history we're told 'there's only one perfect being'
And that's where we can feel the greatness that cannot be seen
*

THERE IS ONLY ONE PERFECT BEING.

Life

***

If you call me your friend, then don't hide your true self from me
Without trying to, the real you will eventually escape for me to see
I will see through the shell of your outside
With all hopes I'll like what's seen on your inside
*

Often we admire other's not knowing what we see might not be real
We judge others from their outside . . . having no idea how it makes them feel
We even look at some and say they're so lucky to have no worries
In fact if you knew their needs, you wouldn't judge in such a hurry
*

They can't eat, sleep or do much without assistance
Would you be happy living that existence?
Would you want with such hungry persistence?
*

If you had many others' life, with another's you wouldn't be consumed
Not being able to read other people's mind, means nobody should assume
Take a look at your life and be thankful for what you do own
Some out there might be looking at you wishing yours was their own
*

No matter how little of it you might see . . .
Yes there might be someone looking wishing . . . like you they could be.

What Would You Do If

***

You see your friend's spouses cheating and think 'what would happen if it was my man'
Using comments as 'I'd leave his ass' . . . But I don't want to test that shoe in my hand
*

That comment, it's easily said. While not wondering if someday she'll be in the same position
Much more so, not thinking if she might already be there . . . but with no idea of the full situation
*

Many put their minds outside . . . concentrating on a fictitious idea of what their man is about
Thinking that a human can be somewhat perfect . . . but not these being . . . without a doubt
Man usually seem to have a way of explaining their own behaviour
Always coming down to 'it's not my fault'. Man is not our saviour
*

*

Some partners track phone calls, whereabouts, friends, then crash their heart
Doing all that won't stop them from doing whatever they wanted from the start
When they cheat, they're not doing it because their love for the spouse died
Not even thinking that it's disrespectful . . . sometimes can't even explain why
*

He's thinking it's that easy 'piece of ass' and it wouldn't hurt anyone
Her last thought is self respect so it's easy to give it to someone
Sometimes not even their action they give a second thought after the act
Many have regret but don't mean it won't happen again . . . and that's a fact
Once another easy 'piece of ass' comes running along
They usually stop thinking again, some aren't strong
*

Some are strong enough to fight the urge . . . but I think they are few
What to do about your cheater . . . usually it's not about love but you
*

Some advice can be listened to but not a command to be taken seriously
Advice/opinion is good, but the results will be lived by you only
No one can say not to go crazy on his ass if it make you feel better . . . but what after
Love make us do crazy things, and a spouse betrayal will cause reaction later
*

A good friend said 'stick with the evil you know' because you might find worse
Good men can do bad things and make bad decisions, sometimes act like your curse
For the women who say they would 'leave his ass'
Make sure you know your story and the cost
Before you pass judgement about what your friends' spouses does
Make sure they don't know more about yours now, and what was.

University Of Life

***

Often we don't recognize our blessings as a blessing until we must face the reality
Not always recognizing the positive but take it for granted because of our negativity
Going further, we forget that from every wrong, we learn something for next time
The mistakes we make are lessons to remind us, that some things shouldn't be repeated and to recognize the sign
If someone does wrong, then the lesson is not to trust that person again
But we should not have to keep our heart covered over in pain.
*

Not only the strong is tested so learn and move on
But only the strong can continue even when the pain is not gone
You can't appreciate the positive without the experience of the negative
This world is a classroom preparing us for what's next to live
*

Life is the university and every experience makes up the textbook.

Betrayal

***

Betrayal is never easily overcome, whether it comes from a family member, friend, or worse, a spouse
Many experienced betrayal in some form at some point in their life, while they thought they were on the right course
*

Sometimes it's not recognized because of where it comes from
*

A betrayed mind will look to a friend as a confidant
If the friend starts with 'if it was me I would do', then you should be careful cause that's not what you want
It's your life that is and will be affected by their decision
You're the one who might see it differently with each reflection
A friend should be supportive . . . help you overcome whatever you're going through
'I will be there for you whatever your decision is', sounds nice even if them saying that is not new
*

A true friend should be there to help you stand strong . . . to hold your hand when you just need quiet
Yes, we look to our spouse for protection but a betrayed heart won't be on a no-pain diet
So theirs would be the hardest of handle . . . also the hardest to decide on
What's next? Infidelity destroys what might not be easily recovered after it's gone
*

We can learn to manage and move on . . . though thought will always be on-guard . . . thoughts of some sought
The disappointment of the act brings an embedded constant reminder that can haunt
*

Anger should not be close when making the choice whether to go or stay
Anger will not allow you to act with a true sense of deciding anyway
Anger is a catalyst in you reacting . . . and things will look different after you calm down
No one should tell a person what to do . . . it's your heart and it shouldn't be treated as if it's a stone.

Everyone should have such a friend . . . that will think only of comforting in the end.

Stolen Sex

***

Many might find stolen sex more exciting than at home . . . which could be insane

The person not thinking who is left at home might be craving the same as they are, but have some sense of restraint

They do without thinking sometime, but expecting others to be perfectly sincere with their heart

Expected the other to be emotionally controlled, but accept sorry to work when they get caught

More likely the sorry comes because of getting caught and not because of the act

Then they go round and round in circles and not admitting to any fact

Many times the pain inflicted is at a very high cost

They get an orgasmic hour without thoughts, of suffering the cost
*

Yes, it's known before-hand that the relationship is temporary, but they still lay it all on the line

Would the cheat be able to handle if their spouse did and think their way? 'It's all fine'

Is an hour of nervous, high intensity, achingly pleasurable satisfaction, stolen from someone else's belongings, worth what you might have to give up?

Some would say 'yes if you don't get caught' and others will say 'no, sometimes we just have to sup-it-up'.

Shivers vs Passion

***

Having sex is easy to do and even those who can't do it well, can do it
Making love to someone you're in love with, is totally different from a one night hit
One touch might be different from the other's touch, when trying to compare
Stolen sex is about getting the end result, the orgasm, without emotional ties to bare
Making love is about our woman/man's feelings and needs becoming the important feel
Pleasing becomes your goal, and satisfying becomes a mission that's ideal
*

A person you care for will most likely be a constant in your life
And will be looking to you to bring them pleasure in their life
The fact is, their thoughts of you should bring a smile
The touch, creating shiver, it's great if forever and not just a while
*

A longer commitment over time will eventually bring a sense of safety along with the shivers
With time it turns into an emotional, interaction, of making love without sex and each is a receiver
The shivers turn into passion from the feelings flowing inside from the heart
A satisfying comfort, knowing that you bring something special with your love from the start
Not just for yourself, it shows depth in how much you care
To have that feeling of trust is irreplaceable, and sincere

*

The outside interaction with stolen sex is fun while it last
But having someone you trust will be there to comfort you is
priceless, without the cost
Once you lose that, recovery is next to impossible
So if you have that love, don't lose it, because you are irresponsible.

Who Is The Strong One

***

Recently someone you love told you 'without me you would be nothing', don't worry
Take a step back. Thrown words of blame come at you, don't worry
Take another step back. You may have heard that 'you won't survive without me'
Take a bigger step back. After you've done so, remind yourself of your inner strength, you'll see
*

The more they try to degrade you, the bigger your steps back, the easier it will be
Keep stepping back until they can't be seen or heard and you're free
Eventually you will feel a sense of relief and peace
So don't think that life is passing you by or seize
*

Remember that they are trying to convince themselves that they don't need you
While they see others available to put up with their crap, only they know might be few
*

When anything negative is said, it's only believed in their head
They're making them self feel better. Now think, soon their thinking will be dead
If you're involved with someone like that,
Then you're the strong one so let nobody take you from that spot
*

Some will say things hoping to scare you into staying nothing
Because they know you are their strength, and if they lose you they'll lose everything

They need you to help them feel secure
Don't confuse their professed love, for you to be more
Know, you really are a need for them to have around
Just don't let them drain your strength, leaving you on the ground
You were given from above for your own purpose
Inner strength is given to make us strong, take care, that's a must

Now use it to nurture you.
And also use it wisely too.

Getting Rid Of Garbage

***

Remember that before you put garbage out
Be sure you won't want it again before tossing it about
Don't think that what's in the bag when thrown is too dirty
Might be dirty to you, but some might not mind filthy
You might remember a clean covering once, but got tarnished over years
The value degrades and it gets handed down as charity, sometimes in tears
*

Never be selfish but know that your used possessions
Might be of great value to someone else, making a transition
Once the value shows signs of degrading
Many step away and start again
By then you are better at recognizing what's good for you
Hopefully, later won't discover that the old is no worse than the new
*

Over time you change your look
Your life becomes a new book
Thinking about it, it isn't easy to say
But the bad feeling can send your mind away
*

Again discovering that around which is tarnished
A relationship, friendship, don't matter as is vanish
Don't allow anyone to control your thought
They're comfortable treating you badly, stay apart
Accepting their treatment, will eventually let you stray

Verona J. Knight

*

If you are compelled to have a brighter future
Push hard to knock them off, don't be their loser
Do not look back and miss out on you success
Because they might have stood in your way of progress

Footnotes of My Mind

Oct 31/12
Closed mind will never see their full capability or the brightest potential in their future.
**

Oct 30/12
It's the hardest thing to show; friendship to someone who doesn't recognize friendship.
**

Oct 27/12
The way I handle a situation is not the perfect way it's only my way, so I try to remember that before I condemn the other person's handling of the same situation.
**

Oct 26/12
Not everything I desire is good and not everything good I desire; whether in food, friends or a man.
**

Oct 25/12
A person is tremendously blessed when they have someone praying for them, especially when they think they don't need praying for.
**

Oct 21/12
It's not every day when you ask 'how are you' that I'll say I'm fine. So if you just ask to be kind, don't, because on that day it might be the day I'll need to take your time and tell you why I'm not.
**

Oct 19/12

Shed a tear then move on; that's good. Shower yourself with tears; only makes them feel good. Set a bath with your tears and your future will be lost; no good. Think of it all as something that's not worth your pain; very good.

**

Oct 19/12

We must be strong enough to know when we need to shed a few tears then move on towards happiness. Never allow our tears to turn into a storm blocking our ability to move on.

**

Oct 14/12

What failed for me might not fail for you. We shouldn't let others failed attempt at something prevent us from trying, just let it teach that 'failed attempts' might come, but finding other ways to do doesn't mean 'failure' must come.

**

Oct 8/12

I'm thankful that my family and I don't have our bad days on the same days. When I have a bad day I'm thankful they can help me catch up to my strength and I can do the same for them on their days.

**

Oct 7/12

We should pray that we don't become the prey for others in our life.

**

Oct 3/12

There are some out there using their body, trying to take that man from his home instead of using it to find one of their own. Remember things changes with time so use it to find better and not to get trapped later.
**

Oct 2/12

'Believe more and then worry less, even though at times worry creates a battle . . . I got to listen more to myself . . . I'm only human but I know my blessings covers me . . . ok remember that . . .' I keep talking to myself.
**

Oct 1/12

Friends goals belong to them as ours belongs to us. Good friends don't need to have the same goals they just need to support each other. So work towards yours and support them with theirs.
**

Sept 21/12

Remember you can't run from yourself because no matter where you go, you will find you there.
**

Sept 20/12

Life has a way of painting pictures for the blind to see the truth. Sooner or later the truth will be shown.
**

Sept 19/12

The loving time we spend with someone is a gift that their memory can unwrap over and over again.
**

Sept 18/12
There comes a time in life when, to keep our sanity, we have to let go of caring about the people who only brings insanity.
**

Sept 17/12
The intelligent side; reads the signs. The curious side; thinks there's more to find. The smart side; knows what to do. But the heart; damn, just won't let them through.
**

Sept 17/12
There are times in life when something hurts your value fast; we give blame saying 'it's because of someone/something that happened in your past'. Find your inner strength and do not allow others to say you are valued low. Never degrade your value using their evaluation. Ignore their voices and go forward using them as motivation.
**

Sept 16/12
We should never mistake that when we give our loyalty that we guarantee getting their loyalty. Loyalty speaks character and yours might be real while theirs is disguise to show as good as yours, but is not.
**

Sept. 14/12
A happy relationship is when each one sees the perfect catch in the other.
**

Sept. 12/12
Just remember that not everyone who say they'll be there for you will pick up the phone when you call in trouble.
**

Sept. 10/12

If someone didn't wish you well in something, just appreciate that they didn't lie to you. Not everyone who says it means it.

**

Sept. 8/12

Never 'lend' what you can't afford to lose and never 'borrow' what you can't afford to give back; including a man.

**

Sept. 7/12

Real love: finding your dreams in each other's reality.

**

Sept. 5/12

The healthiest thing to remember in any relationship is that life doesn't begin and end with the relationship.

**

Sept. 4/12

How many of us are out in the world today actually refurbishing our mistakes in relationships; not learning from the past. Anyone with the same complaints in each of their tomorrow will have the same answer in those tomorrow; they never know the answer if they're searching in the same place where they never found it before.

**

Aug. 29/12

If you did the hurting, then stop telling the person you hurt when they should stop hurting. "I'm sorry" isn't an eraser for the pain. And if you got hurt, then know that "I'm sorry" doesn't mean it might not happen again.

**

Aug. 29/12

Never give advice to someone whose advice you would not use for yourself. And give advice that you would use in a similar situation if given to you by someone else.
**

Aug. 27/12

As humans we all have a past and a future, some past bad some good. And as humans because we don't know our future we shouldn't judge another's bad past; time, sometimes changes plans.
**

Aug. 25/12

Before you admire anyone with their possessions know their story and how it came to be. Would you do the same to achieve it, good or bad?
**

Aug. 24/12

We go from babies through to adults, from creeping to walking, from kindergarten to university. In everything we do, we must move through the learning experiences. This place we know as earth can be the university to whatever is beyond this life before our energy ascends. The way we live might decide whether or not we learned enough to survive the next level. This is just one of my thoughts and a 'what if'.
**

Aug. 19/12

A friendship is a relationship like a marriage is. Both relationships would be more comfortable when we learn the difference between advice and criticize.
**

Aug. 17/12
Damn. If you want to know what a person really thinks of you, wait until you have a fight and listen to them release the brakes off their mouth.
**

Aug. 16/12
The worse disappointment is realizing our mistake of placing someone's standards higher than they can reach it.
**

Aug. 7/12
Many women say there are no good single men out there so they put themselves in relationships with married men, saying 'he's a good man'. News Flash: A married cheat isn't better than a single cheat.
**

Aug. 4/12
Leaving your happiness in someone else's hands will only make you happy when their hands are opened. You'll be giving them too much power over your joy.
**

Aug. 4/12
The names you call a person might say more about you than it does them.
**

July 28/12
A good man wipes your tears away but a great man doesn't cause them.
**

July 25/12

There are times when the Father gives us blessings in disguise but we don't recognize it as one because it's not what we want.
**

July 24/12

At the end of our journey we shouldn't have more regrets about the things we did not do, than for the things we did do.
**

July 23/12

If we don't give ourselves the respect we deserve then others won't either. Self-respect is a tool.
**

July 21/12

Whenever my day starts off rough; depression hits. After thinking, I say 'thank you Jesus'. Why? I know that the Devil don't have to waste time on the ones he already got on his side but he must works hard to ruin the ones who are blessed, so he comes at me. I'm blessed.
**

July 20/12

Make sure who tells you to walk away is not waiting to walk into your spot. Take care in every action.
**

July 17/12

How many times someone said something to us and we heard it totally different from what they meant, having it caused bad feelings in the relationship/friendship. A simple thing as the tone used in a sentence changes the meaning.
**

July 17/12
To lay your heart down for another's married heart to enjoy, is to send your heartache air mail to be delivered at a later date.
**

July 16/12
Those without courage cannot encourage another.
**

July 16/12
When a relationship/friendship/marriage dies, treat it like a funeral. You cry; but not forever. You miss the person; but hold the good memories. You say goodbye; knowing that the life is gone, but remembering that with time your life must go on.
**

July 15/12
It's OK to be selfish once in a while; think about yourself only. But, don't make it a practice.
**

July 15/12
Remember not to serve your love to someone who's not hungry for yours. It should be protected and not given to one who won't appreciate it.
**

July 14/12
Couple of my lessons from relationships so far:
1) Most men usually want a woman more when he knows that he's not 'a need' because she can take care of herself, but she chooses him to share her heart.

2) Most women usually want the man more when she knows she's
   what his heart needs and she isn't just a want; a booty call.

How ironic is that.

**

July 12/12

Stop loving a person for who you want them to be and love them for who you do see. We only get disappointed when we want to change someone who can't be changed.

**

July 11/12

Wolves in sheep clothing will tell you what you want to hear; that way they can have their way with you. They'll never tell you what you need to hear so to help you better yourself, only what you want to hear so to gain your trust, encouraging you to give yourself away.

**

July 10/12

The best revenge is to show your strength. If they bend you use the strength to show them they can't keep you down.

**

July 6/12

A GIRL asks 'you promise you won't hurt me again?' A WOMAN notifies 'I've learned from what you did. It taught me how not to let you hurt me again."

**

July 3/12

"I'm sorry" is not an eraser. The heart is not paper but the pain sticks like ink.

**

July 2/12
My pain of my yesterdays will be my treasures of tomorrow. My best lessons came from my hardest hurt. After the broken bone heals it becomes the hardest part to break again. When the heart heal it's harder to break again.
**

June 27/12
Don't hide your flaws while you work to change them. Shame only gives others power over you since you'll always be on guard of them exposing you.
**

June 26/12
Instead of trying to find the perfect partner, why not find a partner who makes you feel like you are perfect.
**

June 25/12
Stop looking for somebody who's better than the one who broke your heart and find the one whose love is good to you.
**

June 22/12
Never under estimate the power of the words from a liar. But never believe when they say you're nothing. Never under estimate your ability to prove to them they're wrongs. And always feel you must prove your worth only to yourself.
**

June 20/12

The enemies walking behind me brings me no fear. The ones hiding inside my friends are the ones that got me worried.
**

June 19/12

The worse thing that can happen in a relationship is when 'I love you too' becomes a reaction instead of a feeling.
**

June 18/12

Using someone to hurt someone else is only hurting the person you are using. The person you are using has a heart also.
**

June 15/12

If you allow someone to abuse you it only shows that you stop loving yourself before they stopped loving you. Meaning, you never want to see someone you love in pain, so you started hurting you.
**

June 15/12

A real friend knows when you're tired and need some help to be uplifted so to meet up with your strength. Sometimes our strength is just waiting for us to catch up.
**

June 15/12

Weigh the good and the bad in a person before walking away. Even good people do bad things sometimes. Where you see bad, others might be seeing the good and is waiting in line to take on what you throw out. Maybe even the ones telling you to walk away are in that line.
**

June 9/12

There are times when we need to study our partner's actions before we evaluate. Sometimes we use the way we give it to show how we want to get ours. That means the way they give it is how they want to get it. Sometimes their actions speaks louder than what we hear.

**

June 9/12

They say 'love is a battle field' but that's true only if you signed up for the war.

**

May 26/12

Like a piece of coal under pressure, prepare to be a diamond in the end.

**

May 24/12

I'm not perfect by any means but I want to be perfectly smart about my life. Stay away from bullshit and its carriers.

**

May 23/12

Sometimes I do feel like quitting. Usually that stops when my mind is no longer a blur.

**

May 23/12

The answer to feeling good is, just to feel. Sometimes we find ourselves too numb.

**

May 22/12
Playing it safe is sometimes more dangerous than taking a chance but playing it safe means you'll never learn how to solve problems.
**

May 21/12
Sometimes our biggest problem comes in our trust of trusting whom we should trust.
**

May 18/12
Sometimes their bullshit ends up sitting in your lap if you're not careful.
**

May 18/12
Too many run to the church building for protection instead of running to the FATHER. Everything I have comes from my blessings; health, kids, husband, and everything else. I go to a building/church to have company to worship. Going is an action of seeking GOD work, but my guarantor comes from within me.
**

May 18/12
Too many force their religious beliefs on others instead of allowing their lifestyle of bestowed blessings speaks for them.
**

May 17/12
Never be afraid to love. Be afraid if you don't know how to love.
**

May 15/12
The hardest falls can only come from the one we love the most.
**

May 13/12
His/Her love should be inspiring and feels safe. Love shouldn't make you feel like you're walking on egg shells. Love should make us feel secure and safe. Love should make us comfortable to give and receive. Love shouldn't make us feel like we're in the welfare line waiting to collect something.
**

May 12/12
Allow no one to use the words from their lips to scar your hopes and dreams; whether it's from sweeping you off your feet or from trampling your dreams under their feet.
**

May 11/12
Make sure that their 'I'm sorry' is sincere before giving your 'I forgive you'.
Before you say 'I forgive u' accept that sorry might only last till the next time 'I forgive u' is asked for again. Maybe even again and again so make up your mind how many forgiveness you'll give. After the first forgiveness the others carries much pain.
**

May 10/12
Some people are unhappy with themselves only because someone else is unhappy with them. Nobody should need to change to please someone. We should be loved for the real us, and have a real us walk, think, and act as our self. We should appreciate the real us even if others don't.
**

May 8/12
Not everyone say the right words because they mean it, some are only trying to gain your trust.
**

May 5/12
Someone makes degrading comments about you, feel bad for them. They spent all that time studying you to create a comment and people don't examine what they don't think interesting or valuable.
**

May 4/12
Everything we're going through someone already gone through their version of it. You're not alone.
**

May 3/12
Because someone swept you off your feet is no reason to forget your goals so to stop and help them better theirs. Both should support the other to achieve. If it's not that way then the love is going one way.
**

May 2/12
Constantly falling comes with living life; means you're on the move going somewhere. Getting back up is learning; means you know what pain feels like so you're not afraid of the next fall 'forward' to success.
**

April 29/12
If someone stand in the midst of a crowd and an explosion kills all but one, some say it's a miracle he/she survived. Yet the same people can't see the miracle in the fact that they're the only sperm that survived out of millions, so they turn their life a waste of that miracle.
**

April 26/12
Take pride in finding your mistakes. Mistakes means you've made more than one and to get to the next you would've moved from the last; you're moving forward. Mistakes can mean success. Those doing nothing are the ones holding a perfect 'no mistakes' record since they are achieving nothing at a stand-still.
**

April 25/12
The pains caused from my hurdles brings me a better appreciation for my results.
**

April 25/12
Every struggle you are going through . . . every harsh words used to stone you . . . every prayer they pray to bring you failure . . . forced you to find your strength, so let them keep helping your progress, success.
**

April 24/12
Always searching for happiness will make you unhappy. Once you start loving yourself for being you, happiness will come, flow.
**

April 24/12
Revenge doesn't mean you'll spend your time finding ways to hurt them back. Revenge is wasting no time letting them think you must find ways to hurt them back. Ignore them.
**

April 24/12
If we let someone treat us like crap and take our joy, that means we put their worth above ours. In such a case it means we're telling them to treat us how we treat our self; with less value than them.
**

April 23/12
The value I put on others negative criticism of me gives credibility to their sense of my value.
**

April 20/12
What if we stop looking to another for strength and build a reservoir for our own? I think we'd be less dependent and learn to grow stronger while having extra reserve so to help others.
**

April 19/12
It's easy to walk away from a bad relationship but so hard to leave. Walking away is just taking steps, one after the other and another. Leaving is when your heart takes each step with you and not fight to go backwards.
**

April 19/12
Men go bragging about how many women they've slept with and not knowing how many women they left laughing at their backs.
**

April 19/12
Nobody should have to change to make someone else happy. If you knew what you were getting in the beginning you should've walked away then and if you didn't know, don't waste anymore of your time thinking if to stay.
**

April 18/12
It's my choice to be 'not capable of doing' whatever I am not capable of doing.
**

April 18/12
Sometimes the ones we look to for strength are the same ones draining it
the most.
**

April 16/12
Sometimes my mind tells my lips the wrong words. But, it's not because
I'm losing my mind, I'm just pissed.
**

April 16/12
Stop worrying about the past if it done kicked your ass. Work on today
and make sure it doesn't join the kicking line.
**

April 15/12
Because we do something and is not satisfied with the results, it doesn't
mean doing it was a mistake. It will teach you along the way.
**

April 14/12
Without sadness we wouldn't recognize joy and without feeling weakness
we couldn't know our strength.
**

April 13/12
If you're waiting on someone to change for you, it's time to change your
view. Step aside then take another look to see the worth.
**

April 12/12
Too many out there are married to singles.
**

April 11/12

They don't always mean you bad with their actions but that's all they may have experienced.

**

April 10/12

You can't have a better tomorrow if you are constantly thinking about yesterday.

**

April 10/12

I never fear what my enemies plan behind my back. My confidence in the ALMIGHTY already prepared me for their attacks.

**

April 09/12

You can hide your ways from me because I don't matter but can you hide from the CREATOR who does?

**

April 09/12

It's not their secrets that break down the relationship but it's your reaction as a result of finding out; that does . . . .

**

April 08/12

You can't live in tomorrow since by the time it come its already being lived as today. So don't wait for tomorrow to do what you must since only today is a sure thing.

**

April 06/12
A cheat will fall apart if cheated on. An abuser will go crazy if their loved one is abused by another. Do they believe others won't feel the way they do when they commit these acts?
**

April 05/12
Sometimes you see 'friend' in someone while they see 'opportunity' in you. Do not get the two confused.
**

April 4/12
I sometimes wonder how many make love to one's physically while making love to someone else mentally at the same time. Many probably wish they could read minds.
**

April 2/12
If you can't keep your mouth shut about your business why would you get upset if who you told can't either.
**

March 31/12
Because someone tried playing with our dignity is no reason to let them push us to forget our self respect.
**

March 30/12
Fighting to hold on to 'a little' in a relationship means one's willing to settle. If someone is worth the fight then accept it then move forward instead of losing time rehashing. The past didn't make you leave in the first place so why waste time on it.
**

March 28/12
If someone claims credit for your success, look up and say thank you FATHER. He kept you from falling to a personality that wasn't enough to hold your attention to keep you from searching for your success.
**

March 26/12
Abuser: one with low self esteem finding pleasure in physically overpowering an emotionally dependant one.
**

March 25/12
I feel no way about the eyes roaming as long as everything else points home.
**

March 17/12
A spouse who forgives physical abuse out of misplaced love is an abuser of self.
**

March 8/12
Never ask a person without courage for encouragement.
**

Jan 22/12
Stress is a prison. Release yourself and tell yourself you have served your time.
**

Jan 22/12

Sometimes we have people in our life who we don't want to be like. So for 6 days, 24hrs per week, just be who you like.

**

Jan 21/12

Why should I pretend that I'm perfect/almost perfect? My mind said a few choice words to a few people and even though it wasn't vocal some of them heard me through my action. My blessings still comes so I'm not worried.

**

Jan 19/12

Because of the hurdles we sometimes struggle with, we so often see problems as a mountain when there's only a hill.

**

Jan 18/12

What I regret most in life is having reasons to say "I should have done" instead of saying "I did but". I'd rather know that I've done something and didn't get the results I wanted but can do it a different way instead of wondering 'what if'.

**

Jan 17/12

Trying to erasing our past is like trying to erase a university education.

**

Jan 16/12

I plan to de-weed the garden in my mind to see mine and others beauty. To embrace the 'Laws of Attraction' to the fullest and accomplish my goals. Also, to avoid those who wants to derail me.

**

Jan 13/12

I've noticed that to some people, a sin is not a sin when it serves their own purpose.
**

Jan 11/12

If someone is trying to pull you down to their level, step up higher and do them a favour. They'll have to reach higher to get to you; in turn you will be pulling them up.
**

Jan 5/12

Don't say because of your love for someone, you didn't do whatever you needed to. So if you decide not to do something, make the reason be because of your morals.
**

Jan 5/12

It's what surfaces in the light that frightens us more. What stays in the dark is hidden and we don't know it's there to frighten us if it stays unseen. Life.
**

Jan 3/12

Why do the people who have no problem hurting others are the ones least able to handle getting hurt.
**

Jan 3/12

There are times when silence is golden, as it might be more understood than an outstanding speech.
**

Jan 2/12
Our Creator is not materialistic. To attain things/money, that comes with work and hurdles.
**

Jan 1/12
Every time we lift a fork to our mouth or sip from a cup, there's a chance of choking. I've choked before but still must eat. Nobody can ever say they won't eat or drink since the sure thing would be death. If you've been hurt don't say you'll never love again. Take a chance on life and eat love.

****

Why I Write:

. . . I remember going to church one morning and kept hearing the pastor saying 'hold up your hand'. At the time my body was in church but my mind was far away. While I was wherever, I didn't hear the full question but I heard 'hold up your hand' repeated. My mind came back to church to see that the pastor was looking me right in the face since my hand was the only one in the air. Apparently, the question was 'if you think that the Lord has failed you, hold up your hand.'

I left church that day in humiliation. Many things were going wrong in my life at the time and sometimes felt that the Lord failed me and I did nothing to warrant it, but I didn't really meant to hold my hand up.

We often take simple actions lightly. For me that simple hand raising moment got me to think about my life instead of feeling sorry for myself. I started thinking about my accomplishments and needed more to show. Having my children and husband, I still wanted more to show for my life on this earth. I started writing poem, just my thoughts in writing. I had so many feelings flowing and had no way of expressing them or ones to express them to.

The more I put on paper the more my mind gave me to write, so I decide to use characters to say what I wanted to, and I kept writing more. My writing then turned into books in which I created a world where I could say, do, and act without fear of consequences. In these books I expanded the truth far beyond, then embellished the story to match each character.

I finished the books in THE CHEATERS TRILOGY: 'The Cheaters, The Wife, The Revenge', then 'The Cheaters, The Mistress, Her Story' and 'The Cheaters, The Husband, The Payback' in a way to have all three sides of their stories told, using excuses from my life and others to create the characters.

In the novels I made the main character a poet so she can speak my thoughts in the poetry. After finishing the novels, I again, still had thoughts to express so I now present them in my series of books of poetry. To insure that I didn't lose my mind through my trials, I decided to name my books of poetry, A MIND NOT LOST. Each one of the books is a reminder to me of how I found my strength. Each with over 100 pages of poems and thoughts, reminds us of our faith, sexuality and strength. A MIND NOT LOST.

It took me a couple of years to get my answer about my hand raising incident at church. Had I not gone through the painful experiences in my life along with the embarrassment, I wouldn't have achieved my accomplishments, and came out so much stronger than I ever was. My adversities became the rock on which I stood to search for my worth.

My advice to anyone who might have had a same or similar experience is to keep going. Take a rest from searching and look around because sometimes your worth is looking back at you. From my situation I have gotten stronger and I also know that the Lord did not fail me. I want these writings to tell people that our pain was given to teach us strength . . .

ACKNOWLEDGEMENTS:

Relatives and friends who have helped and is helping me with their encouraging words along the way.

SPECIAL THANK YOU:

MY FAMILY for helping me to cope and giving me reasons to still grow. The love you have for each other brings a sense of satisfaction in my heart. I realize how blessed I am and that I've always had my blessings I see today.

ABOUT THE AUTHOR

Verona was taught as a child that a woman should marry, have kids and be happy. As a mother and wife she was happy but not totally satisfied. Her life fell off track when her marriage stumbled over trials she faced, her kids didn't seem to need her attention as much and her health threw her some unexpected curves; she had to face it all at the same time. She found herself in a place where she felt cheated out of happiness.

One day while day-dreaming in church she found herself in an embarrassing moment when the Pastor asked 'if anyone think that the Lord failed you hold up your hand' and when her mind drifted back she found her hand alone in the air; not meaning to. She apparently didn't hear the full question but only heard 'hold up your hand'. That embarrassing moment left her walking out of church with her head low. After that experience she decided to do something about her self-pity; to find herself.

She began writing her thoughts down, good and bad. She started writing a world away from reality; to live through her characters and 'THE CHEATERS TRILOGY' was written with each written from the wife, the mistress and the husband point of view.

Over time she accumulated many thoughts on paper and the end result is a series of poetry. Three books of poetry, 'A MIND NOT LOST' books 1, 2 and 3. Each book containing over 100 pages of poems and thoughts which she wrote to remind herself that through it all she didn't lose her mind and that hand raising moment in church, pushed her to find herself. She has.

A MIND NOT LOST Book One, already on sale. Book Two, now available and Book Three coming soon.

OTHER WORKS BY AUTHOR:

A MIND NOT LOST—Book of Poetry Book 1 and Book 2 (Now on sale)

Books One, Two and Three, each presents a collection of more than 100 pages of poems and thoughts that helped kept me strong and maybe can do the same for you; as others said helped them through. It's my thoughts on paper where I can re-read, to keep boosting my good thoughts and remind me of my strength on a daily basis. My thoughts of the day are included as they are ones that came to mind while observing and thinking about different situations and experiences in mine or friends lives; they have helped me through turmoil times. These thoughts also remind me daily of the strength of my faith, the balance required to soothe each other's mind in a relationship, and of my sexuality.

A Mind Not Lost

Book 1

Verona J. Knight

"THE CHEATERS TRILOGY"

The first of the Trilogy THE CHEATERS THE WIFE THE REVENGE tells the wife's side of the story, the second THE CHEATERS THE MISTRESS HER STORY tells the mistress's side of the story, and the third THE CHEATERS THE HUSBAND THE PAYBACK tells the husband's side.

As it is said, there are three sides to every story. THE CHEATERS TRILOGY tells all three from the Wife the Mistress and the Husband's view of this threesome.

Available in E-book and Paperback

'THE CHEATERS THE WIFE THE REVENGE' (Now on Sale)

This is the first of THE CHEATERS TRILOGY. Tells the story of Jenny, Dwayne's loyal wife and mother of his kids, who finds her marriage in trouble as her husband strays into Sandy's life. Follow Jenny as she uses her detective instincts to uncover the truth while deciding how to face it, then finding ways to deal with her husband and his mistress Sandy. Unhappy with her findings, she tries to put her marriage back together but ends instead finding herself a lover, William, who she wasn't looking for. William now brings her more than she expected or is unsure she wants, starting her on a whole new path.

'THE CHEATERS THE MISTRESS HER STORY'

The second book of THE CHEATERS TRILOGY. Takes you along as Sandy, Dwayne's mistress, find ways to manipulate his love; hoping that along the way she'll be a big enough hunger for him not to be able to do without. Along the way she wants to give him reasons for him to want to leave Jenny and his kids and make her his life. She'll do whatever it takes for him to make her and her kids his family. After she realizes how much she trapped herself, she's also realize that her life is the same as the one she criticizes her twin sister, Sharon, for living. While dealing with Sharon and her problem relationships with her several baby fathers, she also must deal with her cousin Monica who's living on the edge. All this, while dealing with Dwayne's wife who thinks she's too sophisticated to deal with her and her friends who finds it's their business to take care of her.

'THE CHEATERS THE HUSBAND THE PAYBACK'

The third book of THE CHEATERS TRILOGY. Dwayne must now deal with Jenny after she finds evidence of his cheating and keep his relationship with Sandy without putting himself in deeper trouble. Thinking he's man enough to manage them both, he's unable to cope at times and makes mistakes to put him further in but believes he'll be fine since Jenny is too in-love with him to leave him. While denying all of Jenny's accusations and finding ways to prevent the end of his marriage, he knows in his heart that Jenny wouldn't betray him the way he has her. Then one day it all came tumbling down. By the time he finds out about the other man, William, he's already a problem and Dwayne now feels the shoe on the other foot, watching his world falling apart.